PERSONALIZED

FAIRY TALES

ABOUT YOUR CHILD

Boys Edition

ALEKSANDRS POSTS

PERSONALIZED FAIRY TALES ABOUT YOUR CHILD: BOYS EDITION

First edition. June 1, 2023.

Written by Aleksandrs Posts.

Foreword

When I was first introduced to Aleksandrs Posts' manuscript for "Personalized Fairy Tales About Your Child," I was immediately struck by the unique approach to storytelling. The concept of inserting your child's name into the story, making them the hero of their own tale, is both innovative and necessary in today's world where personalized experiences are becoming the norm.

What makes these stories unique isn't just the personalization aspect, but also the core values they impart. Aleksandrs has brilliantly woven elements of empathy, self-confidence, and responsibility into each tale, creating stories that not only entertain, but also educate and inspire.

As a parent and an advocate for children's literacy, I'm always on the lookout for books that will ignite a love for reading in young hearts. "Personalized Fairy Tales About Your Child" does just that, and so much more. It's a book that will create lasting memories for parents and children alike, and I am thrilled to introduce it to you.

Elena Posta, Mother

Preface

Writing this book was a journey that started more than a decade ago, in the heart of bustling summer camps. I observed children's remarkable ability to learn and empathize when presented with stories that mirrored their own experiences. The seed was planted for a book that would take this idea to the next level - personalized fairy tales where the child is the main character.

Years later, as I unpacked a box in my new home, I found my early manuscripts. The world was in the throes of a pandemic, and the need for connection, learning, and escape into the imagination was greater than ever. Slowly, those manuscripts grew into the book you hold today.

"Personalized Fairy Tales About Your Child" isn't just a collection of stories. It's a tool for parents to engage with their children, to teach them important life values, and to show them they are the heroes of their own lives. I hope these stories bring you as much joy to read as they brought me to write.

Happy reading!

Dedicated to...

My loving family, whose unwavering support has been the foundation upon which this book was built.

And to my dear grandmother, who may no longer be with us but will forever remain my guiding light and best friend. Your wisdom, love, and memories continue to inspire me every day.

Thank you all for being the most incredible source of strength and encouragement in my life.

Contents

Introduction

Welcome to a world of enchanting fairy tales, created especially for children and their parents! These 12 chapters, each containing a unique fairy tale, are brimming with love, kindness and valuable life lessons that will gently guide your little ones towards better behavior, overcoming their fears and tackling age-related challenges.

Within these pages, children will learn about responsibility, empathy and self-confidence. These stories will help them navigate life's challenges with grace, instill good manners and encourage truthfulness. As a result, your children will become more helpful, giving you some well-deserved free time.

What sets this book apart is its personal touch! You'll find blank spaces labeled "_____" throughout the tales, ready to be filled with your children's names. This personalization allows your children to feel a deeper connection to the tale and its characters. They'll be thrilled to join the adventures of someone with their name, along with their parents or friends! These personalized tales are not only entertaining but also a powerful way to impart important life lessons.

Three distinct editions – Boys Edition, Girls Edition and Universal Edition – have been created to ensure grammatical correctness and cater to each child's gender identity. While the stories remain the same, the pronouns are adapted to fit the specific edition, such as "he, his" for the Boys Edition and "she, her" for the Girls Edition. The Universal Edition is designed to accommodate families with multiple children, providing an inclusive reading experience for all. By offering these editions, the goal is to create a delightful and engaging experience for every child, making storytime a cherished moment for the whole family.

Before diving into a story, ensure it's suitable for your children. Don't forget to read together in a warm, inviting space that makes everyone feel at ease and happy!

3

Personalized Fairy Tales About Your Child: Boys Edition

CHAPTER 1: When a child spends too much time on their smartphone

_____ and the Quest for the Magical Balance

Long before the world knew the steady march of time, in a place where the earth sang with every breath, there lived a boy named _____. He walked the land with a heart full of wonder, eyes open to the beauty of creation. Yet, in the heart of _____'s vibrant world, a shadow loomed: the captivating allure of the little screen.

_____ found himself increasingly drawn to the fascinating applications on his smartphone, each one more enticing than the last. He became entranced by the endless stream of images, videos and games and the more he swiped and tapped, the deeper he fell into the digital realm.

One day, after spending hours glued to his smartphone, _____'s parents encouraged him to take a break and enjoy some time outside. As he stepped into the garden, the warm sunlight greeted him and he soon felt a gentle breeze that seemed to whisper secrets from faraway lands.

"Dear _____," the breeze murmured softly, "I see you have been captivated by the enchanting world within your smartphone. But there is more to life than what lies behind the screen and I wish to show you the wonders of the world around you."

Intrigued, _____ asked, "How can I find balance between the digital world and the real one?"

The wise breeze replied, "Come with me and I will show you the beauty and magic that exists in both realms."

As they embarked on their journey, the breeze introduced _____ to the fascinating aspects of the digital world – the creativity, knowledge and connections it could offer. But the breeze also guided _____ through the enchanting world outside the screen – the laughter of friends, the songs of birds and the dance of leaves in the wind.

Together, they explored the wonders of both worlds and _____ learned the importance of balance. He realized that while the digital realm held its own unique charm, the enchantment of the world around him was equally important to his happiness and well-being.

From that day on, _____ embraced the beauty of both the digital and the real world. He discovered the key to a truly fulfilling life was finding harmony between the captivating wonders of the screen and the magic of the world beyond.

Discussion Questions:

1. What are some of your favorite activities to do outside that do not involve a smartphone or tablet?
2. Can you think of some advantages of spending time in the digital world and also in the real world?
3. Can you recall something interesting you've learned or discovered on your smartphone or tablet?
4. How do you feel after spending time outside, playing or simply enjoying nature?
5. Why do you think it's important to have a balance between digital and real-world activities?

CHAPTER 2: When a child demands to buy something at the store

_____ and the Enchanted Toy Shop

In a bustling town, there lived a young boy named _____ who loved visiting the local toy shop. The store was filled with all sorts of wonderful and exciting toys, games and gadgets that sparked his imagination.

One day, while exploring the shop with his mother, _____ spotted a particularly fascinating toy that he simply had to have. He pleaded with his mother to buy it for him, but she gently explained that they couldn't afford it at the moment and that sometimes it was important to be patient and save for the things we truly desire.

Feeling disappointed, _____ reluctantly left the store without the toy. As he walked away, he noticed an old man sitting on a nearby bench, watching him with a curious smile.

"Hello, _____," said the old man. "I couldn't help but notice your love for that toy in the store. I know it's hard to wait, but sometimes there are more important things in life."

Confused but intrigued, _____ asked the old man what he meant.

"Let me show you," the old man said with a grin. He waved his hand and suddenly they were standing in front of an enchanted toy shop. It was filled with the most extraordinary toys _____ had ever seen and each one seemed to be alive with magic.

The old man explained, "In this shop, the toys have the power to grant your deepest wishes, but only if you're willing to offer something in return. You must give up something you cherish, learn a valuable lesson or perform a selfless act."

Excited, _____ eagerly agreed to the challenge. He went through a series of tasks: first, he helped an elderly woman carry her groceries; next, he shared his favorite toy with a younger child who didn't have any; and finally, he volunteered to clean up the park to make it more beautiful for everyone to enjoy. Each task taught him a valuable lesson about patience, gratitude and the importance of giving back to others.

After completing the tasks, _____ returned to the enchanted toy shop. The old man congratulated him on his success and granted him a special toy that would remind him of the lessons he had learned.

When _____ returned home with the toy, he found that he no longer felt the need to possess every new toy he saw. Instead, he cherished the magical toy and the memories of his incredible adventure.

As time went by, _____ grew into a thoughtful and generous young man, always mindful of the lessons he had learned in the enchanted toy shop. He shared his experiences with others, inspiring them to appreciate the true value of the things they had and to always be patient and considerate in their desires.

Discussion Questions:

1. Can you think of a time when you wanted something very much like _____ wanted the toy? How did it make you feel?
2. Why do you think it's important to sometimes wait for things we really want?
3. Can you think of a kind or selfless act you could do for someone else, like _____ did in the enchanted toy shop?
4. How would you feel if you were in _____'s position, learning lessons from the enchanted toy shop? What would you do differently?

5. How would you feel if you were in ____'s position, learning lessons from the enchanted toy shop? What would you do differently?

CHAPTER 3: When a child overeats sweets

_____ and the Land of Never-ending Sweets

In a world where the sun always seemed to shine a little brighter, there lived a curious child named _____. He was known for his boundless energy and endless curiosity. However, he had one weakness – his insatiable love for sweets.

One day, as _____ was walking home from kindergarten, he stumbled upon a mysterious, hidden path. He couldn't resist following it and it led him to a magical land filled with sweets of every

14

kind: towering mountains of chocolate, rivers of caramel and trees bearing cotton candy leaves.

Excited by this delightful discovery, _____ immediately began to indulge in this sugary paradise. He ate and ate, unable to resist the allure of these never-ending sweets. Hours passed and the sun began to set. _____ ate so many sweets that his stomach began to hurt and he realized that it was time for him to go home.

As he started to leave the land of sweets, a wise old gingerbread man appeared before him. "_____," he said, "you have learned an important lesson today. Sweets can be enjoyable, but only when consumed in moderation. Your tummy ache is a gentle reminder that too much of a good thing can be harmful."

The gingerbread man continued, "Remember, balance is key. Now, take this magical candy cane and it will show you the way home." _____ took the candy cane and the sweet land began to fade away as he retraced his steps back to the hidden path.

Upon arriving home, _____ was greeted by his worried parents. He told them all about his journey to the land of never-ending sweets and the lesson he had learned. From that day on, _____ enjoyed sweets responsibly, always keeping in mind the wise words of the gingerbread man.

And so, young _____ grew to be healthy and strong, understanding the importance of balance in life and he shared his story with other children, teaching them the valuable lesson he had learned in the Land of Never-ending Sweets.

Discussion Questions:

1. Can you tell me about a time when you ate a lot of sweets, like _____ did? How did it make you feel?
2. What do you think about _____'s experience in the Land of Never-ending Sweets? Would you

have done anything differently if you were there?

3. Why do you think it's important to have a balanced diet and not eat too many sweets?

4. How would you explain the lesson that _____ learned to a friend?

5. How do you think _____ felt when he came home and told his parents about his journey?

CHAPTER 4: When a child does not like to get up early

How _____ learned to wake up early in the morning

In a quaint village, where the sun greeted the rooftops every morning, lived a boy named _____. He was known for his cheerful and adventurous spirit. But there was one thing that _____ struggled with – waking up early in the morning.

Each day, _____'s parents would gently try to rouse him from his slumber, but he would grumble and pull the covers over his head, wishing to stay in his cozy bed.

One starry night, as _____ slept soundly, a radiant dream enveloped him. He found himself standing on a cloud at the edge of a fantastical realm, where the sun had yet to rise. Beside him stood a kind, glowing figure named Aurora, the Guardian of Dawn.

"_____," Aurora said softly, "I have brought you here to show you the beauty and magic that unfolds when the day begins. Perhaps this will inspire you to fall in love with the sunrise."

With a wave of her hand, the sky above them started to transform. Hues of pink, orange and gold painted the horizon, casting a warm and gentle light on the world below. Creatures of the land began to stir, greeting the new day with delightful songs and dances.

_____ watched in awe as the once dark and sleepy landscape became vibrant and full of life. He saw the shimmering dewdrops on the grass, the busy bees collecting nectar from the flowers and the rabbits frolicking in the meadows.

As the sun continued to rise, Aurora turned to _____ and said, "See, young one, the dawn holds a unique enchantment that can only be experienced by those who rise early. Now, it's time for you to return to your world, carrying with you the magic of the morning."

When _____ awoke, he could still feel the warmth and wonder of the dawn he had witnessed in his dream. Eager to experience it again, he sprang from his bed and rushed outside, greeted by the first light of day.

From that day on, _____ began to appreciate the beauty and magic of the early morning. He embraced waking up with the sun and as he did, he discovered a newfound energy and excitement for each new day.

Discussion Questions:

1. How do you feel when you have to wake up early in the morning? Do you think _____ felt the same way?
2. What do you think was the most beautiful part of the sunrise that _____ saw in his dream?
3. Why do you think Aurora, the Guardian of Dawn, wanted to show _____ the sunrise?
4. How do you think _____ felt when he woke up and remembered his dream?
5. How might waking up early help _____ in his everyday life? How could it help you?

CHAPTER 5: When a child does not want to sleep apart

_____ and the Magical World of Dreams

In a land far, far away, where rolling hills stretched as far as the eye could see and laughter filled the air, there lived a young boy named _____ with his loving family. _____ was a creative and adventurous child, but he had one small problem - he didn't want to sleep apart from his parents.

Each night, as his parents tucked him into his cozy bed, _____'s imagination would start to run wild. He would worry about being alone in his room and would plead with his parents to let him sleep in their bed.

One starry evening, a gentle breeze swept through _____'s window, carrying with it a mysterious and enchanting creature – the Dream Weaver. The Dream Weaver, with a warm and friendly smile, introduced herself to _____.

"Dear _____, I've heard about your fears of sleeping alone and I'm here to help you. Tonight, I will take you on a journey to the magical world of dreams, where you'll discover the wonders that await you in your sleep," she said, her voice soothing and melodious.

Excited yet nervous, _____ agreed to go on the adventure. Hand in hand with the Dream Weaver, they floated through the window and into the mystical night sky.

Together, they visited dreamlands filled with whimsical landscapes, vibrant colors and friendly creatures. _____ played with talking animals, soared through the sky on the back of a dragon and even built magnificent sandcastles on the shores of a dreamy ocean.

As the journey continued, _____ began to understand the beauty and importance of sleep. The Dream Weaver showed him how all child's dreams were connected, creating a vast web of shared imagination and wonder.

By the end of the adventure, ____'s fears of sleeping alone had vanished. They returned to his bedroom and the Dream Weaver gently tucked him in.

"Remember, ____, when you sleep, you're never truly alone. You're connected to the world of dreams and all the friends you've made there," she whispered before disappearing into the night.

From that day on, ____ looked forward to bedtime, excited to explore the magical world of dreams each night. He felt comforted knowing that even in sleep, he was surrounded by friends and adventures, never truly alone.

Discussion Questions:

1. How does _____ feel about sleeping in his own bed at the start of the story? Can you relate to this feeling?
2. How do you think _____ felt when he first met the Dream Weaver?
3. What were some of the exciting things _____ got to see and do in the dreamlands? Which one would you want to experience?
4. How did visiting the dreamlands help _____ overcome his fear of sleeping alone?
5. How do you think _____ feels about bedtime now? Do you think you might feel the same way if you visited the dreamlands?

CHAPTER 6: When a child is afraid of the dark

The Magical Adventure of Brave _____

Once upon a time, in a cozy village close to a beautiful forest, there lived a young boy named _____. He was curious and loved going on adventures, spending his days playing happily with his friends. But _____ had a secret: he was scared of the dark.

Every evening, when the sun went to sleep and the moon took its place, shadows seemed to turn into scary monsters hiding in the corners. Shivering with fear, _____ would hide under his warm blanket.

One sunny day, while playing in a grassy clearing near the forest, _____ saw a wise old owl sitting on a branch, watching him. Confused, _____ wondered why the owl, a nighttime bird, wasn't sleeping. As he carefully walked closer to the owl, it began to speak with a gentle voice:

"Hello, _____. I know you're scared of the dark, but tonight, I'll show you that darkness can be your friend."

_____ looked at the owl, surprised and curious. "A friend?" he asked softly.

"Yes," the owl answered kindly. "Darkness can be a place full of fun and adventures if you learn to see it that way. So, tonight, I'll take you on a journey through the night and you'll see the magic that can be found in the dark."

Feeling both excited and a little nervous, _____ agreed to go on the journey. As night fell, he lay in his bed, waiting for the owl. Soon enough, the owl arrived and together they started their magical adventure.

As they flew above the forest, the darkness sparkled with the light of fireflies, making everything glow softly. The stars in the sky shone brightly like little treasures. The wind shared gentle secrets and the night fairies sang calming songs.

As they travelled through this wonderful world, _____ felt his fear slowly disappear, replaced by happiness and amazement.

After their journey, the owl brought _____ back home, wishing him a good night's sleep. As the owl flew back to the forest, its wing touched the window and the sound woke _____ up. Opening his eyes, he saw that a bright, sunny morning had come.

From that day on, _____ wasn't afraid of the dark anymore. He learned that sometimes the things we're most scared of can turn out to be the most amazing and magical experiences.

Discussion Questions:

1. How did ＿＿＿ feel about the dark at the beginning of the story? Can you recall a time when you felt the same way?
2. What did the owl promise to show ＿＿＿? How do you think ＿＿＿ felt about this?
3. Can you describe some of the things ＿＿＿ experienced during his journey through the night? Which part do you find the most magical?
4. How did ＿＿＿'s feelings towards the dark change after his adventure with the owl?
5. What lesson do you think ＿＿＿ learned from his adventure? How can you apply this lesson to your own fears?

CHAPTER 7: When a second child is born in a family

_____ and the Little Star

In a warm and loving home, a young boy named _____ lived happily with his parents. He was their pride and joy, and they cherished every moment spent with him.

One day, _____'s parents shared some exciting news – a new baby was on the way! _____'s heart swelled with anticipation and he eagerly awaited the arrival of his new sibling.

As the days passed, his parents prepared the home for the baby, painting a new nursery and buying tiny clothes and toys. They talked to _____ about what it meant to be a big brother and the important role he would play in the baby's life.

Finally, the day arrived when the little bundle of joy came into the world. _____'s parents introduced him to his new sibling, a baby girl they named Viola. She was like a tiny, shining star that had fallen from the sky into their family.

At first, everything seemed perfect. _____ was thrilled to be a big brother and he loved watching Viola sleep, playing with her and taking care of her. But as the days went by, _____ began to feel a twinge of jealousy. His parents were spending so much time caring for Viola that he felt left out and lonely.

Sensing _____'s feelings, his parents sat down with him and explained that, while Viola needed their attention as a newborn, they still loved him just as much as before. They reassured him that he would always be their special boy and that they were proud of the loving big brother he was becoming.

_____'s parents also encouraged him to find ways to bond with his baby sister. He could read her stories, sing her lullabies or even just talk to her about his day. As he spent time with Viola, _____ discovered that he could be her protector, her teacher and her friend.

Slowly, the jealousy in his heart began to fade, replaced by a deep sense of love and responsibility for his little sister. The family grew stronger and their love for one another blossomed like a beautiful garden.

Years passed and as Viola grew, the bond between the siblings only deepened. _____ taught her how to ride a bike, tie her shoelaces and even how to face her fears. In turn, Viola looked up to her big brother with adoration and gratitude and together, they shared countless adventures and cherished memories.

As they grew older, _____ and Viola became the best of friends, always supporting and caring for one another. They knew that no matter what challenges life might bring, they would face them side by side, bound by the love and understanding that only siblings can share.

And so, _____ learned that the arrival of a new baby in the family was not a reason for jealousy, but rather a chance to experience the wonder and joy of a love that would last a lifetime.

Discussion Questions:

1. How did _____ initially feel about becoming a big brother? How did his feelings change after Viola was born?
2. Can you understand why _____ might have felt left out and lonely when his parents were spending a lot of time with Viola? Have you ever felt similar feelings?
3. How did _____'s parents help him understand and deal with his feelings of jealousy?
4. What activities did _____ do to bond with his little sister? Can you think of some activities you could do with a younger sibling or a friend?

5. What lesson did _____ learn from his experience of becoming a big brother? How do you think this lesson might apply to you?

CHAPTER 8: When a child takes someone else's things

_____ and the Enchanted Box of Treasures

Many years ago, in a place where time seemed to stand still, a young boy named _____ spent his days filled with laughter and adventure. _____ had a kind heart and loved to play with his friends, but one day, he stumbled upon a problem he had never encountered before.

One sunny afternoon, while playing near the coast, _____ found a mysterious box, adorned with colorful gems and intricate carvings. Curiosity piqued, he opened it and discovered an assortment of fascinating trinkets inside. Without thinking, he took the box home, eager to explore its contents further.

Later that day, _____'s best friend, Lily, came over to play. As they were playing, Lily noticed the box and exclaimed, "That's my grandmother's enchanted box of treasures! We've been looking for it everywhere!"

_____ realized he had taken something that didn't belong to him. He wanted to make things right, but he didn't know how.

As the sun began to set, a gentle knock on the door caught their attention. Standing there was a wise old woman, the village storyteller.

"_____, I know you didn't mean any harm when you took the box, but it's important to understand that taking someone else's belongings is not right," she said, her voice filled with kindness and understanding.

The wise woman then shared an enchanting tale about a magical kingdom where every person's belongings had unique powers and taking something that didn't belong to you would disrupt the balance of the entire land.

As _____ listened, he began to understand the importance of respecting others' belongings and the consequences of taking what wasn't his. Moved by the tale, he knew what he had to do.

With a sincere heart, _____ returned the enchanted box of treasures to Lily and her grandmother. Lily and her grandmother forgave _____ and they started tea together with a delicious cake.

From that day on, _____ became more mindful of others' belongings and the entire village learned a valuable lesson about respect, forgiveness and the magic of understanding.

Discussion Questions:

1. How did _____ feel when he first found the enchanted box of treasures? Why do you think he decided to take it home?
2. When Lily recognized the box, how do you think _____ felt? Have you ever been in a situation where you realized you made a mistake?
3. How did the wise woman's story help _____ understand his mistake? Can you remember a story that helped you understand something better?
4. What did _____ do to correct his mistake? How do you think this made Lily and her grandmother feel?
5. After this experience, how do you think _____ will behave the next time he finds something that doesn't belong to him? What lesson have you learned from _____'s story?

CHAPTER 9: When a child is dishonest with parents

_____ and the Mysterious Island of Truth

In a faraway kingdom, where the golden sun kissed the rolling hills and the crystal-clear river murmured sweet lullabies, a boy named _____ lived in a quaint little cottage with his loving family. The picturesque kingdom was a sanctuary of love and laughter and _____'s days were filled with  endless adventures and warm embraces. Yet, sometimes his curiosity led him to make choices that weren't quite right - he had developed a habit of being dishonest with his parents.

One warm afternoon, as _____ walked along the riverbank, he stumbled upon a small, peculiar stone that shimmered like the stars. Intrigued, he picked it up and discovered that the stone could speak.

"Hello, _____," said the stone with a gentle voice. "I am the Stone of Truth and I have noticed that you sometimes struggle with honesty. Come with me to the Mysterious Island of Truth and I will help you find the path to honesty and trust."

Curious, _____ agreed to be guided by the Stone of Truth. The stone then led him through calm waters to a hidden island shrouded in mist. Having set foot on the Mysterious Island of Truth, where honesty was the key to discovering the wonders of the world, their magical adventure began.

In this enchanting island they encountered various challenges that required _____ to be truthful, even when it was difficult. The Stone of Truth guided _____ through each challenge, helping him understand the importance of honesty and the consequences of deceit.

The first challenge involved _____ admitting a recent time when he had lied to his parents. As he spoke the truth, a once-barren tree bloomed with beautiful flowers. The second challenge required _____ to tell the truth about a situation where he had been dishonest with a friend. As he confessed, a bridge appeared, allowing them to cross a wide chasm. In the third and final challenge, _____ had to promise to always strive for honesty in his future actions. As he made this promise, a dazzling rainbow appeared across the sky, symbolizing the beauty that honesty could bring to the world.

As _____ and the Stone of Truth navigated this magical island, he came to realize that honesty not only strengthened his relationships with others but also filled him with a sense of pride and self-confidence.

At the end of their journey, the Stone of Truth congratulated _____ on his newfound understanding of the value of honesty. As a reward, the Stone of Truth gifted _____ a small seed, which would grow into a tree that would always remind him of the lessons he had learned on the Mysterious Island.

As they returned to the kingdom, _____ and his parents planted a seed in their cottage yard. Over time it grew into a magnificent tree full of green leaves and large sweet oranges. Colorful parrots often flew around the tree that stood as a symbol of honesty and trust and sang their songs about the kind and honest _____.

Discussion Questions:

1. Can you tell me why the Stone of Truth took _____ to the Mysterious Island? What do you think he learned there?
2. In the story, _____ had to admit to times when he wasn't honest. How do you think he felt during those moments? How would you feel in his place?

3. ____ made a promise to always strive for honesty. Why do you think this promise is important? Would you like to make a similar promise?
4. The seed from the Stone of Truth grew into a tree in ____'s yard. What do you think this tree symbolizes? What would be your symbol of honesty?
5. How can you use what ____ learned about honesty in your own life? Can you think of a situation where being honest is important?

CHAPTER 10: When a child needs guidance on treating animals

_____ and the Magical Creature's Quest

In a quaint village nestled in the heart of a lush valley, there lived a young boy named _____. He was a spirited child who enjoyed exploring the surrounding woods and meadows. However, he hadn't yet learned the importance of being gentle with the creatures he encountered.

One sunny day, while wandering through the forest, _____ stumbled upon a small creature with shimmering wings.

Excited, he reached out to grab it, but in his haste, he accidentally hurt the creature, causing it to let out a faint cry of pain.

Feeling guilty, _____ realized the consequences of his actions and decided to seek help from the wise old woman who lived on the outskirts of the village. She was known for her knowledge of magical creatures and their secrets.

As _____ approached her hut, the wise woman heard the boy's footsteps and invited him in. He explained what had happened and she listened intently.

"_____, it's essential to treat all living beings with kindness and respect," she said gently. "But I see that you are truly sorry, so I will give you a chance to make amends."

The wise woman handed _____ a small, enchanted bottle filled with healing elixir. "You must return to the forest and find the creature you hurt. Offer it this elixir and it will heal its wounds. Along the way, you will learn the importance of compassion."

Determined to make things right, _____ set out on his journey to find the injured creature. He encountered many animals and magical beings, each with their own stories and lessons. They taught him the importance of empathy, understanding and caring for all living things, no matter how big or small.

After several days, _____ finally found the creature he had hurt. Its wings were still frail and it looked at him with cautious eyes. _____ gently offered the healing elixir and as the creature drank it, its wings began to shimmer and heal.

Filled with gratitude, the creature revealed itself to be a guardian of the forest, capable of bestowing blessings upon those who showed kindness to its inhabitants.

As a reward for his compassionate journey, the guardian blessed _____ with a newfound connection to nature, allowing him to understand the feelings and needs of all living beings.

_____ returned to his village, a changed boy. He shared his experience with his friends and family, teaching them the value of kindness and respect for all creatures. From that day on, _____ became a friend to all living beings and continued to nurture the delicate balance of the magical world around him.

Discussion Questions:

1. How did you feel when _____ first found the magical creature and accidentally hurt it? What would you have done differently?
2. Why do you think the wise woman gave _____ the healing elixir? Can you think of any ways we can help animals that might be hurt or in danger?
3. _____ learned a lot from the animals and magical beings he met on his journey. What is one lesson you think is important to remember when dealing with animals?
4. How did _____'s behavior towards the magical creature change by the end of the story? Can

you think of a time when you changed your behavior after learning something new?

5. In the end, _____ became a friend to all living beings. How can we show kindness and respect to the animals we encounter in our daily lives?

CHAPTER 11: When a child doesn't like to wash up

_____ and the Battle of the Dirt Monsters

Once upon a time, in a delightful little house nestled between the trees, lived a young child named _____. He enjoyed exploring the nearby woods and fields with his friends, engaging in all sorts of adventures. However, there was one thing that _____ didn't like – washing up.

Every day, after playing outside, _____'s parents would remind him to wash his hands and face, but he would grumble and try to avoid it. Little did he know that soon, he would discover a reason to appreciate cleanliness.

One evening, after a day filled with fun and play, _____ went to bed without washing up. As he fell asleep, his vivid imagination took over and carried him into a dreamland. In this dream, _____ found himself standing in the center of his beloved village, but something was amiss. The whole village was covered in dirt and strange creatures roamed the streets. These creatures were the Dirt Monsters.

Just as _____ started to feel frightened, a bright, shimmering light appeared before him and a gentle voice whispered, "_____, only you can save the village from these Dirt Monsters. They are here because of the dirt that has accumulated. To banish them, you must use the power of cleanliness."

As the light faded away, _____ noticed a golden bucket filled with sparkling water and a soft cloth by his side. Remembering the gentle voice's message, he bravely approached the first Dirt Monster, dipped the cloth in the water and started to clean it. As the dirt disappeared, so did the creature, dissolving into a harmless puff of dust.

Encouraged by this success, _____ continued to clean the village, scrubbing away the dirt and grime that covered the streets, the houses and even the trees. He battled each Dirt Monster with determination, using the power of cleanliness to drive them away.

As he wiped away the last bit of filth, the village transformed back into its beautiful, pristine state. The residents, who had been hiding from the Dirt Monsters, emerged from their homes, clapping and cheering for _____.

Upon waking up, _____ realized that his dream had taught him an essential lesson: cleanliness was not only a way to stay healthy but also a powerful force that could protect his loved ones and his village. From that day on, _____ embraced washing up with enthusiasm, knowing that he was a valiant guardian against the Dirt Monsters.

Discussion Questions:

1. How did you feel when _____ entered his dreamland and saw the Dirt Monsters? What would you have done if you were in his place?
2. In the story, the Dirt Monsters represented the dirt and germs that we carry when we don't wash up. Can you think of other reasons why it's important to keep ourselves clean?
3. What did _____ use to get rid of the Dirt Monsters in his dream? How does this relate to real-life cleanliness practices?
4. How did _____'s attitude towards washing up change after his dream? Can you think of a time when you changed your mind about something after learning more about it?
5. How can you help remind others about the importance of cleanliness, just like _____ did after his dream adventure?

CHAPTER 12: When a child doesn't want to cut his nails

_____ and the Enchanted Clippers

In a time long ago, in a small village nestled between rolling hills, lived a young boy named _____. He was a cheerful and spirited child, with a head full of dreams and a heart full of love for his family and friends.

_____ had many talents and interests, but there was one thing he disliked: cutting his nails. Every time his parents tried to trim them, he would squirm and protest, making it nearly impossible to get the task done.

One sunny afternoon, while playing at the edge of a nearby forest, _____ stumbled upon an old, worn-out chest. Curious, he opened it to find a pair of gleaming golden nail clippers adorned with intricate engravings. They seemed almost magical and _____ couldn't resist taking them home.

That night, as his parents prepared to cut his nails once again, _____ presented the golden clippers to them. His mother and father exchanged puzzled glances but decided to give them a try.

As the golden clippers touched _____'s nails, something magical happened. The clippers seemed to hum a soothing melody and _____ felt a warm, calming sensation that made him feel at ease. For the first time, he sat quietly, allowing his parents to trim his nails without any fuss.

His parents were amazed by the transformation and thanked the enchanted clippers for their help. From that day on, nail trimming became a peaceful and enjoyable experience for the entire family.

Over time, _____ began to understand the importance of good hygiene and self-care. He realized that keeping his nails neat and clean was a small yet essential part of maintaining his overall health and well-being.

The golden clippers continued to serve _____ and his family faithfully, never losing their magic touch. They became a cherished heirloom, passed down through generations, reminding each child of the importance of self-care and the power of a little magic to transform even the most mundane tasks into enchanting experiences.

And so, young _____ learned that sometimes, even the smallest acts of care could make a big difference in one's life and that a little magic could be found in the most unexpected places.

Discussion Questions:

1. How did you feel when _____ found the enchanted clippers? Were you surprised to discover their magical powers?
2. In the story, the golden clippers helped _____ feel comfortable while getting his nails cut. Can you think of something that could make this task easier for you?
3. Why do you think it's important to keep our nails neat and clean? How does this relate to our overall health and well-being?
4. How did _____'s attitude towards cutting his nails change after his experience with the magical clippers? Can you think of a time when your feelings about something changed after trying it?
5. How can you make daily self-care tasks, like cutting nails, more enjoyable? What would be your 'enchanted clippers' for these tasks?

How 'Personalized Fairy Tales About Your Child' Came to Life

About ten years ago, I worked in a summer camp, and it was there that I stumbled upon a pretty fascinating discovery. I found that children seemed to absorb lessons more deeply when they were part of a story, especially a story that mirrored their own lives. This got me thinking, and I started jotting down a few ideas. But then life happened, I moved houses, and the drafts got lost in the shuffle.

Fast forward to 2020, a year none of us are likely to forget. During the lockdown, I found those old drafts in a forgotten box. Reading them again, I was struck by the potential of my old idea. As the world slowed down, I began to write, and the pages of my manuscript slowly but surely began to multiply.

Now, writing a book isn't as easy as it sounds. It took time, patience, and many cups of coffee. But as I worked, an idea began to form. What if the story was not just about any child, but about a specific child - the one hearing the story? That's when I decided to create a personalized book, a unique story starring your child.

But here's the thing - I realized that to make the tales feel truly personal, I needed to be mindful of the child's identity. My family suggested creating separate editions for boys and girls, allowing for the correct use of pronouns. And so, the idea of three editions - one for boys, one for girls, and a universal version - was born.

And now, after all the brainstorming, writing, and editing, I'm thrilled to announce that on this International Children's Day, 1st of June 2023, 'Personalized Fairy Tales About Your Child' is ready to share its magic. I can't wait for you and your children to step into these unique adventures. I've poured my heart into these books, and I hope they'll bring you joy and create wonderful shared memories.

About the Author

Aleksandrs Posts, the visionary behind "Personalized Fairy Tales about Your Child," is a seasoned global explorer and internationally recognized trainer with a deep-seated passion for igniting young minds and facilitating their growth. As the chairman of the Latvian Youth Development Center, Aleksandrs has accumulated a wealth of experience engaging  with young adults via international education programs and camps. His educational background in business psychology and a certificate in experiential education serve to enhance his proficiency in this domain.

Leveraging his profound knowledge of psychology, education, and a multitude of cultures, Aleksandrs weaves enchanting, instructive, and culturally rich fairy tales for children. His narratives aim to nurture positive behavior, alleviate fears, and imbue a sense of responsibility, empathy, and self-confidence in young readers. Aleksandrs is a firm believer in the transformative power of fairy tales as potent instruments for imparting invaluable life lessons and shaping character.

With a rich background in EU lobbying and training, Aleksandrs has refined his communication skills and his prowess in conveying compelling key messages. His dexterity in crafting captivating and impactful learning experiences shines through in his writing. His narratives are both engaging and leave a deep, lasting imprint on readers. As an advocate for the nurturing of young minds, Aleksandrs is devoted to delivering unforgettable stories that encourage strong bonds between parents and children. It is his hope that his personalized fairy tales will serve this noble purpose.

Ingram Content Group UK Ltd.
Milton Keynes UK
UKHW010652050623
422889UK00005B/810